# muffins

Ivy Press

# muffins

## 25 mouthwatering recipes

Stephanie Evans

First published in 2008 by

**Ivy Press**
The Old Candlemakers
West Street, Lewes
East Sussex BN7 2NZ, UK
www.ivy-group.co.uk

ISBN-13: 978-1-905695-73-7
ISBN-10: 1-905695-73-X

Printed in China

10 9 8 7 6 5 4 3 2 1

**Ivy Press**
This book was conceived, designed
and produced by Ivy Press.

*Creative Director* Peter Bridgewater
*Publisher* Jason Hook
*Editorial Director* Caroline Earle
*Art Director* Clare Harris
*Senior Editor* Lorraine Turner
*Senior Art Editor* Sarah Howerd
*Project Designer* Joanna Clinch
*Publishing Assistant* Katie Ellis
*Concept Design* 'Ome Design
*Photographer* Jeremy Hopley
*Food Stylist* Susanna Tee

# contents

# introduction

**Making muffins is what people think of as 'comfort cooking' – a welcome task when it's cold outside, or first thing on a weekend when you don't want to disturb the relative domestic calm.**

A batch of muffins is also ideal to meet the after-school urgency for a tasty treat. They are made and baked quickly, from a few simple ingredients, and the results always hit the spot. Like pancakes, muffins probably began as a way of using store cupboard ingredients to produce something filling. The basic batter is simple to make, using baking powder and/or bicarbonate of soda and, sometimes, buttermilk or soured cream. The trick is not to overwork the mixture – too smooth, and you lose the light texture – so go for about 15 seconds mixing: how's that for fast food? They are quicker than bread and just as delicious for teatime as they are for a leisurely breakfast or a lunch with salad and cheese. They satisfy kids on the go and are a great way to get some fruit, vegetables or nuts into their diet, as well as getting them involved in the kitchen.

Muffins are not cakes and they don't have to be sweet or rich; some of the brunch ideas go fine with bacon or smoked salmon, and the plainer spiced ones are delicious with a wedge of cheese or a piece of fresh fruit on picnics or at the end of a meal. They are great for feeding a crowd – you could even serve tiny versions as canapés with drinks.

We love muffins for their homely appeal, usually served when still warm, but sometimes a blob of thick cream, home-made jam or lemon curd doesn't go amiss. They don't really need decoration, but if making them as a gift, for kids' parties or annual festivals such as Easter or Halloween, you can dress them up appropriately. There are a few decorating ideas on page 62 to get you started.

# the basics

You need little in the way of equipment or experience to make muffins and a batch can be prepared in less than 10 minutes. Make sure you preheat the oven, and position a couple of shelves in the top and centre.

You certainly don't need fancy food-processors or mixers; in fact, overworking is death to a good muffin. A fork to beat the liquid ingredients and a wooden spoon for stirring everything roughly are fine. You want a large jug or bowl for the wet stuff and a big mixing bowl for the dry. I sift the dry ingredients twice to combine the raising agents and to maximise the air in the mixture.

Quality bakeware significantly adds to the pleasure of cooking. These days, we've got some canny inventions to make turning out and clearing up afterwards as easy as pie. Silicone muffin trays and individual cases are great. Try to buy a selection of different sizes to cover all occasions and all appetites. If you want non-stick metal pans, buy the best you can afford: Circulon® is recommended.

Paper cases make muffins perfect for popping into a lunchbox or picnic basket. You can also make your own by cutting out discs or squares of baking paper, about 5 cm/2 in larger in diameter than your muffin pan size. Scrunch the paper slightly, then oil and line the insides.

## Useful tips

• The fan setting on an electric oven is too drying for muffins – avoid it if you have the option – or put a shallow tray filled with very hot water on the bottom of the oven to keep the air moist. Large muffins will cook in 20–30 minutes, but smaller ones need checking after 15 minutes.

• If you are using silicone muffin pans, cooking times may be slightly shorter than with metal ones, so do check.

• If eating muffins warm, give them 5 minutes out of the oven to set and to allow some ingredients such as chocolate and dried fruits to cool slightly.

• If you want to ice or decorate muffins, leave them on a cooling rack to cool completely before doing so.

• Muffins are best eaten the day they're made.

• If you are making more than one tray of muffins at a time you may need to swap their places in the oven so that they cook evenly, but it's fine to open the oven door as they cook; muffins don't sink like soufflés do.

# a feast of muffins

### brunch classics

blueberry

maple syrup

saffron

polenta

raspberry

caraway

parmesan

chilli and olive

dill and seed

### teatime treats

peanut butter

citrus

pecan fudge

dried cranberry

chocolate date

ginger

apricot

coconut

pumpkin

### muffin sensations

teenyweeny

cherry

beetroot

sticky toffee

chocolate swirl

marzipan

spiced orange

# blueberry muffins

For many of us, the quintessential muffin is made with plump, juicy blueberries, and there's no doubting their appeal, especially when the berries burst and ooze a little juice.

## makes 12

### you will need

oil, for greasing

300 g/10½ oz plain flour

150 g/5½ oz granulated sugar

2 tsp baking powder

pinch of salt

2 eggs

½ tsp vanilla extract

1 carton (284 ml/10 fl oz) buttermilk

75 g/2¾ oz butter, melted

100 g/3½ oz fresh or frozen blueberries

icing sugar, for dusting

1 Preheat the oven to 200°C/400°F/Gas Mark 6. Lightly grease a 10- or 12-hole non-stick muffin tray or line with paper cases.

2 Sift together the dry ingredients. Whisk the eggs, vanilla extract, buttermilk and melted butter together in a large mixing bowl. Quickly stir the dry ingredients into the whisked mixture, but don't try to blend smoothly; the batter should be a little lumpy. Add the blueberries, trying not to break them.

3 Spoon the batter into the prepared tray or cases almost to the top. Transfer to the oven and bake for about 20 minutes, or until the muffin tops are well risen and springy to the touch. Test one by inserting a skewer into the centre to check it comes out clean.

4 Remove the muffins from the oven and allow to cool in the tray for 5 minutes, then transfer to a wire rack. Dust with sifted icing sugar before serving.

# maple syrup muffins

Maple syrup adds a smoky sweetness redolent of pancakes or waffles. Serve these warm with butter for breakfast. I like to add sultanas to the batter, but you can omit them if you prefer.

**you will need**

350 g/12 oz plain flour

2½ tsp baking powder

pinch of salt

2 eggs

zest and juice of 1 lemon, plus up to 4 tbsp semi-skimmed milk (depending on size and juiciness of lemon)

200 ml/7fl oz buttermilk

75 g/2¾ oz butter, preferably unsalted, melted

5–6 tbsp maple syrup, plus extra for drizzling

60 g/2¼ oz sultanas

1 Preheat the oven to 200°C/400°F/Gas Mark 6. Line a 10- or 12-hole non-stick muffin tray with paper cases.

2 Sift together the dry ingredients. Whisk together the eggs, lemon zest and juice, buttermilk, butter, 5 tablespoons of maple syrup, and the milk if using, in a large mixing bowl. Quickly stir the dry ingredients into the whisked mixture, but don't try to blend smoothly. The batter should be quite runny; if it seems too dry, add another tablespoon of maple syrup. Lightly stir in the sultanas; again, do not overmix.

3 Spoon the batter into the prepared cases almost to the top. Transfer to the oven and bake for 20–25 minutes, or until the tops are well risen and springy to the touch. Test one by inserting a skewer into the centre to check it comes out clean.

4 Remove the muffins from the oven and allow to cool in the tray for 5 minutes, then transfer to a wire rack. Drizzle with extra maple syrup while still warm.

# saffron muffins

These muffins offer a delicious trio of flavours, with the pine kernels adding a pleasing crunch. They are good with a wedge of cheese, or simply eaten with butter and extra honey.

## makes 12

**you will need**

oil, for greasing

5 tbsp runny honey

5 tbsp sunflower oil

good pinch of saffron strands (about 30)

300 g/10½ oz plain flour

2 tsp baking powder

½ tsp bicarbonate of soda

½ tsp salt

2 eggs

200 ml/7 fl oz buttermilk or Greek yoghurt

50 g/1¾ oz soft brown sugar

75 g/2¾ oz pine kernels

25 g/1 oz porridge oats

1 Preheat the oven to 200°C/400°F/Gas Mark 6. Lightly grease a 10-hole non-stick muffin tray or line with paper cases.

2 Measure out the honey and oil into a small jug and stir in the saffron. Set aside to infuse.

3 Sift together the dry ingredients. Whisk the eggs, buttermilk and sugar together in a large mixing bowl, then incorporate the saffron-infused honey and oil. Add the pine kernels and porridge oats. Quickly stir the dry ingredients into the whisked mixture, but don't try to blend smoothly, and do not overmix – it will be quite runny.

4 Spoon the batter into the prepared tray or cases almost to the top. Transfer to the oven and bake for 20–25 minutes, or until the tops are well risen and springy to the touch. Test one by inserting a skewer into the centre to check it comes out clean.

5 Remove the muffins from the oven and allow to cool in the tray for 5 minutes, then transfer to a wire rack.

# polenta muffins

This recipe came about when I found I'd almost run out of flour. The golden-coloured polenta is gorgeously enhanced by using orange juice and zest, so this muffin is the obvious choice for breakfast, with marmalade.

## makes 10–12

**you will need**

olive oil, for greasing

100 g/3½ oz plain flour

150 g/5½ oz polenta flour

2 tsp baking powder

½ tsp bicarbonate of soda

50 g/1¾ oz caster sugar

50 g/1¾ oz desiccated coconut

1 egg, beaten

½ tsp orange flower water or vanilla extract

grated rind and juice of
1 orange, made up to 200 ml/
7 fl oz with semi-skimmed milk

75 g/2¾ oz butter, preferably unsalted, melted

shredded zest of 2 oranges, to decorate

1   Preheat the oven to 200°C/400°F/Gas Mark 6. Lightly grease a 10-hole non-stick muffin tray or line with paper cases.

2   Sift together the dry ingredients into a large bowl twice, to ensure the raising agents thoroughly combine with the polenta. Mix the egg with the orange flower water, orange rind and juice, and milk. Stir in the cooled melted butter. Quickly stir the whisked mixture into the dry ingredients just to combine – no more than 20 seconds.

3   Spoon the batter into the prepared tray or cases almost to the top. Transfer to the oven and bake for about 20 minutes, or until the tops are well risen and springy to the touch. Test one by inserting a skewer into the centre to check it comes out clean.

4   Remove the muffins from the oven and allow to cool in the tray for 5 minutes (or remove paper cased ones immediately). Transfer to a wire rack and sprinkle with shredded orange zest.

**Tip:** Polenta is gritty compared with wheat flour. Try whizzing the polenta in a blender to make it as fine as possible.

# raspberry muffins

The tartness of raspberries is perfect in a muffin. Use firm fresh fruit if you can, but frozen berries can be substituted (add them frozen, otherwise they will be too soggy).

## makes 12

### you will need

oil, for greasing

300 g/10½ oz plain flour

2 tsp baking powder

½ tsp bicarbonate of soda

½ tsp salt

175 g/6 oz golden granulated sugar

150 ml/5 fl oz soured cream

150 ml/5 fl oz buttermilk

2 eggs

75 g/2¾ oz butter, preferably unsalted, melted

100 g/3½ oz fresh or frozen raspberries

fresh raspberries and cream, to serve

1 Preheat the oven to 200°C/400°F/Gas Mark 6. Lightly grease a 12-hole non-stick muffin tray or line with paper cases.

2 Sift together the flour, baking powder, bicarbonate of soda and salt. Whisk the sugar, soured cream, buttermilk, eggs and butter together in a large mixing bowl. Quickly stir the dry ingredients into the whisked mixture, but don't try to blend smoothly. Lightly stir in the raspberries; again, do not overmix – the batter should be a little lumpy.

3 Spoon the batter into the prepared tray or cases almost to the top. Transfer to the oven and bake for about 25 minutes, or until the muffin tops are well risen and springy to the touch. Test one by inserting a skewer into the centre to check it comes out clean.

4 Remove the muffins from the oven and allow to cool in the tray for 5 minutes, then transfer to a wire rack. Serve with raspberries and cream.

# caraway muffins

A savoury muffin that needs little else: split and spread with a little butter or soft cheese and maybe a crisp apple to munch on. The seeds give an appealing speckle and texture.

## makes 10–12

### you will need

oil, for greasing

300 g/10½ oz plain flour

2 tsp baking powder

½ tsp salt

pinch of sugar

pinch of powdered cumin (optional)

4 tsp caraway seeds or poppy seeds

115 g/4 oz butter, melted

150 ml/5 fl oz soured cream

150 ml/5 fl oz semi-skimmed milk

sea salt, for sprinkling

1  Preheat the oven to 190°C/375°F/Gas Mark 5. Lightly grease a 10- or 12-hole non-stick muffin tray or line with paper cases.

2  Sift together the dry ingredients and stir in the caraway seeds. Whisk the butter, soured cream and milk together in a large mixing bowl. Quickly stir the dry ingredients into the whisked mixture, but don't try to blend smoothly.

3  Spoon the batter into the prepared tray or cases almost to the top and lightly sprinkle with sea salt. Transfer to the oven and bake for about 25 minutes, or until the tops are well risen and springy to the touch. Test one by inserting a skewer into the centre to check it comes out clean.

4  Remove the muffins from the oven and allow to cool in the tray for 5 minutes, then transfer to a wire rack.

# parmesan muffins

How about breakfast with an Italian twist? Alternatively, make these as mini muffins to serve with drinks. If you don't fancy the garlic, try a teaspoon of chopped fresh oregano leaves instead.

## makes 10–12

### you will need

**150 g/5½ oz Parmesan, in one piece**

**300 g/10½ oz plain flour**

**2 tbsp baking powder**

**½ tsp salt**

**125 ml/4 fl oz olive oil, plus extra for greasing**

**1 small egg**

**200 ml/7 fl oz buttermilk**

**175 ml/6 fl oz semi-skimmed milk**

**1 garlic clove, finely chopped**

1  Preheat the oven to 200°C/400°F/Gas Mark 6. Lightly grease a non-stick muffin tray or line with paper cases.

2  Cut off about a fifth of the Parmesan and grate it finely. Set aside. Coarsely grate the remainder.

3  Sift together the dry ingredients. Whisk the oil, egg, buttermilk and milk together in a large mixing bowl. Quickly stir the dry ingredients into the whisked mixture, but don't try to blend smoothly. Lightly stir in the coarsely grated Parmesan and the garlic; again, don't overmix.

4  Spoon the batter into the prepared tray or cases almost to the top. Transfer to the oven and bake for about 15 minutes. Remove the tray from the oven and quickly sprinkle with the reserved lightly grated Parmesan. Return to the oven for a further 10 minutes, or until the Parmesan has melted, and the muffins are well risen and springy to the touch. Test one by inserting a skewer into the centre to check it comes out clean.

5  Remove the muffins from the oven and allow to cool in the tray for 5 minutes, then transfer to a wire rack.

# chilli and olive muffins

Great munched warm for a quick lunch. While the muffins are in the oven, you can whip up some salad and slices of mozzarella, or try making mini ones and serving them with drinks.

you will need

**oil, for greasing**

**400 g/14 oz plain flour**

**2 tsp baking powder**

**2 pinches of salt**

**1 pinch of sugar**

**½ tsp finely chopped fresh medium-hot green chilli**

**8–10 green olives, stoned and chopped**

**2 eggs**

**1 carton (284 ml/10 fl oz) buttermilk**

**75 g/2¾ oz butter, melted**

**3–4 sun-dried tomatoes (either in oil or mi-cuit), finely chopped**

1  Preheat the oven to 200°C/400°F/Gas Mark 6. Lightly grease a non-stick muffin tray or line with paper cases.

2  Sift together the dry ingredients, then stir in the chilli and olives. Whisk the eggs, buttermilk, and butter together in a large mixing bowl. Quickly stir the dry ingredients into the whisked mixture, but don't try to blend smoothly; the batter should be a little lumpy. Add the chopped tomatoes and lightly stir to incorporate.

3  Spoon the batter into the prepared tray or cases almost to the top. Transfer to the oven and bake for about 20 minutes for regular or 10–12 minutes for minis, or until the muffin tops are well risen and springy to the touch. Test one by inserting a skewer into the centre to check it comes out clean.

4  Remove the muffins from the oven and allow to cool in the tray for 5 minutes, then transfer to a wire rack.

# dill seed muffins

The dill and horseradish combination makes these muffins an obvious partner for smoked salmon or mackerel pâté. You could use a little rye flour instead of all wheat, for a northern European flavour.

**you will need**

oil, for greasing

300 g/10½ oz plain flour

2 tsp baking powder

½ tsp bicarbonate of soda

¼ tsp salt

2 tsp dill seeds

75 g/2¾ oz butter, melted

100 ml/3½ fl oz soured cream

1–2 tsp creamed hot horseradish

200 ml/7 fl oz semi-skimmed milk

1 Preheat the oven to 190°C/375°F/Gas Mark 5. Lightly grease a 6- or 12-hole non-stick muffin tray or line with paper cases.

2 Sift together the dry ingredients and the dill seeds. Whisk the butter, soured cream, horseradish and milk together in a large mixing bowl. Quickly stir the dry ingredients into the whisked mixture, but don't try to blend smoothly.

3 Spoon the batter into the prepared tray or cases almost to the top. Transfer to the oven and bake for about 20 minutes, or until the tops are well risen and springy to the touch. Test one by inserting a skewer into the centre to check it comes out clean.

4 Remove the muffins from the oven and allow to cool in the tray for 5 minutes, then transfer to a wire rack.

5 Serve bagel-style, with smoked salmon and cream cheese with a teaspoonful of horseradish stirred through it, or try with smoked mackerel pâté.

# peanut butter muffins

This recipe was inspired by the sandwich combination made famous by Elvis Presley, because I found all-banana muffins too sweet. Overripe banana is fine, by the way!

## makes 10–12 (6 large)

### you will need

oil, for greasing

1 large or 2 small bananas

1 tsp lemon juice

1 heaped tbsp crunchy peanut butter

150 g/5½ oz plain flour

150 g/5½ oz granulated sugar

2 tsp baking powder

pinch of salt

2 eggs

1 carton (284 ml/10 fl oz) buttermilk, or semi-skimmed milk

50 g/1¾ oz unsalted butter, melted

### to serve

dulce de leche (from a jar)

50 g/1¾ oz unsalted peanuts, roughly chopped

1 Preheat the oven to 190°C/375°F/Gas Mark 5. Lightly grease a 6- or 12-hole non-stick muffin tray or line with paper cases.

2 Peel and mash the banana with the lemon juice. Blend in the peanut butter.

3 Sift together the dry ingredients, twice, in a large mixing bowl. Whisk the eggs, buttermilk and cooled butter together in a large mixing bowl, then stir through the banana and peanut butter mixture. Quickly stir the dry ingredients into the whisked mixture for about 15 seconds; don't try to blend smoothly.

4 Spoon the batter into the prepared tray or cases almost to the top. Transfer to the oven and bake for about 20 minutes, or until the tops are well risen and springy to the touch. Test one by inserting a skewer into the centre to check it comes out clean.

5 Remove the muffins from the oven and allow to cool in the tray for 5 minutes, then transfer to a wire rack. Spread a teaspoon of dulce de leche over the top of each muffin and sprinkle with chopped peanuts before serving.

# citrus muffins

If you can stretch to serving homemade lemon curd with these, you're in for a treat. You don't have to use buttermilk in this recipe, with all the citrus juice, semi-skimmed milk can be substituted.

## makes 10–12

### you will need

300 g/10½ oz plain flour

150 g/5½ oz caster sugar

2 tsp baking powder

pinch of salt

finely grated zest and juice of 1 large lemon and 1 lime

1 egg

200 ml/7 fl oz buttermilk

75 g/2¾ oz butter, preferably unsalted, melted

### to serve

2 tbsp lemon juice

5 tbsp caster sugar

finely grated zest of 1 lemon

or

lemon curd, preferably homemade

1 Preheat the oven to 200°C/400°F/Gas Mark 6. Line a 10- or 12-hole non-stick muffin tray with paper cases.

2 Sift together the dry ingredients. Whisk together the lemon and lime zest and juice with the egg, buttermilk and butter in a large mixing bowl. Quickly stir the dry ingredients into the whisked mixture, but don't try to blend smoothly; the batter should be a little lumpy.

3 Spoon the batter into the prepared cases almost to the top. Transfer to the oven and bake for about 20 minutes, or until the tops are well risen and springy to the touch. Test one by inserting a skewer into the centre to check it comes out clean.

4 To serve, make a lemon drizzle sauce by gently heating the lemon juice and sugar without boiling for about 3 minutes. Spoon over the hot muffins and top with the zest. Alternatively, slice off the top third of your muffins, spread with a little lemon curd and replace the lids.

# pecan fudge muffins

Do use paper cases for this one, to catch the melting fudge. For extra indulgence, serve with chunks of even more fudge. You can drizzle with maple syrup or make a simple fudge icing and top with pecan nuts.

makes 8–10

### you will need

150 g/5½ oz plain flour

½ tsp baking powder

pinch of salt

1 large egg

50 g/1¾ oz Demerara sugar

50 g/1¾ oz butter, melted

125 ml/4 fl oz buttermilk

150 g/5½ oz pecan nuts, roughly chopped

25 g/1 oz soft fudge, cut into small cubes, plus extra to serve

### icing

50 g/1¾ oz butter

70 g/2½ oz icing sugar

1 tsp vanilla extract

1 Preheat the oven to 200°C/400°F/Gas Mark 6. Line a 12-hole non-stick muffin tray with paper or silicone cases.

2 Sift the dry ingredients into a large bowl.

3 Whisk together the egg, sugar, butter and buttermilk in a separate bowl. Sift the dry ingredients on top of the egg mixture. Quickly stir together, but don't try to blend it to a smooth consistency. Lightly fold in two-thirds of the pecan nuts and the cubed fudge; again, don't overmix.

4 Spoon the batter into the prepared tray or cases almost to the top. Transfer to the oven and bake for about 20 minutes, or until the tops are well risen and springy to the touch. Test one by inserting a skewer into the centre to check it comes out clean.

5 Remove the muffins from the oven, transfer them to a wire rack and leave to cool. To make the icing, melt the butter in a small saucepan, tip in the icing sugar and stir quickly. Remove from the heat as soon as it bubbles, add the vanilla extract and beat hard until smooth. Use immediately because it sets fast. Sprinkle with the remaining pecan nuts.

# dried cranberry muffins

You don't have to include sesame seeds, but I think they make a nice addition to these muffins – they add extra flavour and colour contrast. You could also use chopped blanched almonds, folded in with the cranberries.

## makes 8–10

**you will need**

oil, for greasing

115 g/4 oz dried cranberries

150 g/5½ oz plain flour

1 tsp baking powder

50 g/1¾ oz caster sugar

¼ level tsp salt

1 egg, beaten

125 ml/4 fl oz semi-skimmed milk

2 tbsp Greek yoghurt

50 g/1¾ oz butter, melted

½ tsp almond extract

2 tbsp sesame seeds, plus extra for sprinkling

1 Preheat the oven to 200°C/400°F/Gas Mark 6. Lightly grease a 10- or 12-hole non-stick muffin tray or line with paper cases.

2 Lightly dust the cranberries in a little flour (you can do this by putting the cranberries in a sieve and shaking the measured flour through the sieve into a large bowl). Now sift the remaining dry ingredients into the bowl.

3 Whisk together the egg, milk, yoghurt, butter and almond extract in a separate bowl. Sift the dry ingredients on top of the egg mixture. Quickly stir together, but don't try to blend it smoothly. Fold in the dusted cranberries and the sesame seeds; again, don't overmix.

4 Spoon the batter into the prepared tray or cases almost to the top. Sprinkle the tops with sesame seeds. Transfer to the oven and bake for about 20 minutes, or until the tops are well risen and springy to the touch. Test one by inserting a skewer into the centre to check it comes out clean.

5 Remove the muffins from the oven and allow to cool in the tray for 5 minutes, then transfer to a wire rack.

# chocolate date muffins

Most muffins don't need dressing up, but these are especially good with a smooth covering of ganache, which is simple to make using equal quantities of chocolate and cream.

**you will need**

**100 g/3½ oz good-quality milk chocolate, broken into pieces**

**200 g/7 oz plain flour**

**25 g/1 oz cocoa powder**

**1 tsp baking powder**

**½ tsp salt**

**115 g/4 oz soft brown sugar**

**2 eggs**

**225 ml/8 fl oz semi-skimmed milk**

**100 ml/3½ fl oz vegetable oil**

**50 g/1¾ oz pitted dates, chopped**

ganache topping

**50 g/1¾ oz good-quality milk chocolate, broken into pieces**

**50 ml/2 fl oz double cream**

1 Preheat the oven to 200°C/400°F/Gas Mark 6. Line a 10- or 12-hole non-stick muffin tray with double paper cases. Melt the chocolate in a heatproof bowl over a pan of simmering water. Stir, then set aside to cool.

2 Sift together the flour, cocoa powder, baking powder and salt. In a large mixing bowl, whisk together the sugar, eggs, milk and oil. Gradually stir in the cooled melted chocolate. Quickly stir in the dry mixture, but don't blend smoothly; the batter should be a little lumpy. Lightly mix in the chopped dates.

3 Spoon the batter into the tray or cases almost to the top. Bake for 20 minutes, or until risen and springy to the touch. Test one by inserting a skewer into the centre to check it comes out clean. Remove from the oven, leave for 5 minutes in the tray, then transfer, still in their cases, to a wire rack to cool.

4 For the topping, melt the chocolate and cream in a small pan over a very low heat. When melted, beat with a wooden spoon until smooth and shiny. Pour a little on top of each muffin (slice the tops to the level of the paper cases, or add a swirl of ganache to each one and let it run down the sides).

# ginger muffins

I made these muffins with ground ginger first, but it didn't give the kick that using freshly grated root ginger does – give it a try! The addition of chocolate complements the ginger, making these muffins a firm favourite.

## makes 12

### you will need

50 g/1¾ oz fresh root ginger, peeled

150 g/5½ oz soft brown sugar

1 tbsp lemon juice

75 g/2¾ oz butter, melted

200 g/7 oz plain flour

25 g/1 oz cocoa powder

1 tsp baking powder

½ tsp salt

2 eggs

1 carton (284 ml/10 fl oz) buttermilk

50 g/1¾ oz crystallised ginger, finely chopped, plus extra to decorate

100 g/3½ oz good-quality dark chocolate, broken into pieces

1 Preheat the oven to 200°C/400°F/Gas Mark 6. Line a 10- or 12-hole non-stick muffin tray with paper cases. Finely grate the root ginger; use a Microplane if you have one. Mix it into the sugar, lemon juice and melted butter in a bowl.

2 Sift together the dry ingredients several times so that the cocoa is evenly distributed through the flour. Whisk the ginger mixture, eggs and buttermilk in a large mixing bowl. Stir in the chopped crystallised ginger. Quickly stir in the dry mixture, but don't blend smoothly; the batter should be a little lumpy.

3 Spoon the batter into the tray or cases almost to the top. Bake for 20 minutes, or until risen and springy to the touch. Test one by inserting a skewer into the centre to check it comes out clean. Remove from the oven, leave for 5 minutes in the tray, then transfer, still in their cases, to a wire rack to cool.

4 Melt the chocolate in a heatproof bowl over a pan of simmering water. Stir, then remove from the heat. Pour over the muffins and leave to set (slice off a little of the tops if any have risen too high). When almost firm, top each with a small piece of ginger.

# apricot muffins

Ground almonds keep the texture moist and make a natural pairing with the apricots in this recipe. Omit the powdered ginger if you prefer. Try serving these muffins with a little jam or honey.

**makes 10–12**

**you will need**

oil, for greasing

200 g/7 oz self-raising flour

150 g/5½ oz ground almonds

2 tsp baking powder

½ tsp powdered ginger

5 tbsp runny honey

¼ tsp almond extract

75 g/2¾ oz butter, preferably unsalted, melted

2 eggs

225 ml/8 fl oz buttermilk or semi-skimmed milk

50 g/1¾ oz dried apricots (no soak), finely chopped

10 whole blanched almonds, to decorate

1  Preheat the oven to 200°C/400°F/Gas Mark 6. Lightly grease a 12-hole non-stick muffin tray or line with paper cases.

2  Sift together the dry ingredients twice. Whisk the honey, almond extract, butter, eggs and buttermilk together in a large mixing bowl. Quickly stir the dry ingredients into the whisked mixture, but don't try to blend smoothly. Finally, add the apricots and stir to incorporate lightly.

3  Spoon the batter into the prepared tray or cases almost to the top. Top each with a blanched almond. Transfer to the oven and bake for about 20 minutes, or until the muffin tops are well risen and springy to the touch. Test one by inserting a skewer into the centre to check it comes out clean.

4  Remove from the oven, leave for 5 minutes in the tray, then transfer to a wire rack to cool.

# coconut muffins

This recipe is altogether darker and richer than most of the other muffins included in this book. The coconut and carrot keep the texture moist, while there is plenty of crunch in the nuts.

you will need

oil, for greasing

50 g/1¾ oz carrot, very finely grated

50 g/1¾ oz desiccated coconut

25 g/1 oz chopped hazelnuts

150 g/5½ oz plain flour

50 g/1¾ oz brown flour

3 tsp baking powder

150 g/5½ oz soft brown sugar

pinch of salt

60 g/2¼ oz butter, melted

3 eggs

125 ml/4 fl oz buttermilk

1 tsp vanilla extract

4 tbsp sunflower oil

to decorate (optional)

toasted desiccated coconut

runny honey, to glaze

1   Preheat the oven to 190°C/375°F/Gas Mark 5. Lightly grease a 6-hole non-stick muffin tray. Mix the carrot, coconut and hazelnuts in a bowl. Sift together the dry ingredients twice into a large separate bowl. Whisk the butter, eggs, buttermilk, vanilla extract and oil in a large bowl. Gently stir in the carrot mixture. Add the whole lot to the dry mixture and lightly combine.

2   Spoon the batter into the prepared tray almost to the top. Transfer to the oven to bake. After 10 minutes, spread the coconut (if using) on a small baking tray and place on the bottom shelf of the oven, under the tray of muffins. Watch the coconut carefully; you just want it to take on colour, not burn.

3   After about 20 minutes, or when the tops are well risen and springy to the touch, remove the muffins from the oven. Test one by inserting a skewer into the centre to check it comes out clean.

4   Leave them in the tray for 5 minutes, then transfer to a wire rack to cool. If you want to decorate them, brush lightly with a little warmed runny honey and sprinkle with the toasted coconut.

# pumpkin muffins

Apart from its gorgeous colour, pumpkin gives a lovely taste and texture to the muffins, sweetened here with apple and warm cinnamon. The nuts are optional, as is the dried fruit.

**you will need**

oil, for greasing

200 g/7 oz pumpkin or butternut squash, peeled weight

1 dessert apple (about 125 g/ 4½ oz), cored and finely diced

2 tsp lemon juice

small handful walnut pieces or dried fruit (optional)

275 g/9½ oz plain flour

3 tsp baking powder

175 g/6 oz soft brown sugar

1–2 tsp cinnamon

1 tsp salt

2 eggs

50 ml/2 fl oz buttermilk

150 ml/5 fl oz sunflower oil

75 g/2¾ oz  butter, preferably unsalted, melted

1 Preheat the oven to 160°C/325°F/Gas Mark 3. Lightly grease a 6- or 12-hole non-stick muffin tray or line with paper cases.

2 Finely grate the pumpkin and mix with the apple in a bowl with the lemon juice to stop it browning. Add the walnuts if using.

3 Sift together the dry ingredients into a large bowl. Whisk the eggs, buttermilk, oil and butter together in a large bowl. Lightly stir in the pumpkin and apple and mix evenly. Quickly stir the dry ingredients into the whisked mixture, but don't try to blend smoothly; you should have a dryish batter.

4 Spoon into the prepared muffin tray or cases and transfer to the oven. Cook for about 25–30 minutes for large ones or 20 minutes for medium.

5 Remove the muffins from the oven and allow to cool in the tray for 5 minutes, then transfer to a wire rack.

# teenyweeny muffins

There is always an appeal in miniatures, especially for kids' parties. Instead of one big cake, try making platefuls of tiny muffins. You could decorate them in advance, or have the guests personalise their own (see page 62).

## makes 48 miniatures

### you will need

300 g/10½ oz plain flour

2 tsp bicarbonate of soda

pinch of salt

300 ml/10 fl oz vegetable oil

300 g/10½ oz soft brown sugar

2 eggs

juice of 2 oranges, made up to 300 ml/10 fl oz with milk

2 tbsp chocolate strands

### to decorate

sugar glaze (2 tbsp granulated sugar, 1 tbsp water)

hundreds and thousands, dragées, chocolate strands or buttons, mini orange slices, or candles

1 Preheat the oven to 180°C/350°F/Gas Mark 4. Place truffle-sized paper cases inside mini muffin trays.

2 Sift together the dry ingredients twice, in a large bowl. In a jug or second bowl, beat together the oil, sugar, eggs, orange juice and milk. Stir in the chocolate strands, then lightly and quickly add the flour mixture. Use a teaspoon to fill the cases almost to the top.

3 Bake in the middle of the oven (if two trays do not fit side by side, bake in batches) for 10–15 minutes. Test one by inserting a cocktail stick into the centre to check it comes out clean. Meanwhile, make a sugar glaze by heating the sugar and water together in a small pan until the sugar melts.

4 Remove the muffins from the oven and allow to cool for a couple of minutes in the tin, then carefully lift out the paper cases onto a wire rack. Quickly brush sugar glaze over the top of each muffin. Sprinkle with hundreds and thousands, dragées or chocolate strands, or top each one with a chocolate button, mini orange slice, or candle.

# cherry muffins

I used dark chocolate to make these less sweet (perfect with a mid-morning cup of coffee). You can, of course, use milk chocolate or a mixture of dark, milk and white chocolate chips.

you will need

**200 g/7 oz self-raising flour**

**pinch of salt**

**60 g/2¼ oz cocoa powder**

**200 g/7 oz soft brown sugar**

**100 g/3½ oz chocolate chips or dark chocolate, coarsely chopped**

**50 g/1¾ oz best glacé cherries, rinsed and quartered**

**75 g/2¾ oz butter, melted**

**200 ml/7 fl oz buttermilk (or use half buttermilk and half milk)**

**1 egg, beaten**

**10–12 whole glacé cherries, to decorate**

1 Preheat the oven to 200°C/400°F/Gas Mark 6. Line a 12-hole non-stick muffin tray with paper cases.

2 Sift together the dry ingredients into a large bowl. You may need to do this several times to get the cocoa powder evenly mixed in; all to the good, the muffins will be lighter! Add the chocolate chips and chopped cherries and stir so that the cherries are coated in the flour mixture. Whisk the butter, buttermilk and egg together in a second bowl. Sift the dry mixture over the top and quickly stir into the whisked mixture, but don't try to blend smoothly.

3 Spoon the batter into the prepared cases almost to the top. Transfer to the oven and bake for 15–20 minutes, or until the tops are well risen and springy to the touch. Test one by inserting a skewer into the centre to check it comes out clean.

4 Remove the muffins from the oven and allow to cool in the tray for 5 minutes, then transfer to a wire rack and top each muffin with a whole cherry to decorate.

# beetroot muffins

These muffins are no shrinking violets – they are striking in both colour and in taste, making them ideal as a Halloween treat. Muffins using vegetables are deliciously moist, but the chocolate doesn't go amiss.

**you will need**

175 g/6 oz cooked beetroot, peeled

50 ml/2 fl oz buttermilk

150 g/5½ oz plain flour

40 g/1½ oz cocoa powder

175 g/6 oz golden granulated sugar

2 tsp baking powder

¼ tsp salt

1 large egg

75 ml/2½ fl oz natural yoghurt

50 g/1¾ oz butter, melted

100 g/3½ oz fresh blackberries

icing sugar, for dusting

1 Preheat the oven to 190°C/375°F/Gas Mark 5. Line a 10- or 12-hole non-stick muffin tray with silicone or paper cases. Finely grate or mash the beetroot into a bowl and mix in the buttermilk to take on the colour.

2 Sift together the dry ingredients. Whisk the egg, yoghurt and butter in a large bowl. Stir in the beetroot and buttermilk and combine to distribute the colour. Quickly stir the dry ingredients into the whisked mixture, but don't try to blend smoothly. Lightly stir in the blackberries; again, don't overmix.

3 Spoon the batter into the prepared tray or cases almost to the top. Transfer to the oven and bake for about 15 minutes, or until the tops are well risen and springy to the touch. Test one by inserting a skewer into the centre to check it comes out clean. Remove the muffins from the oven and transfer in their cases to a wire rack to cool.

4 Once cooled, dust with sifted icing sugar. For a suitably spooky look, you could decorate the tops by dusting them with sifted icing sugar through a stencil shape cut out of baking paper.

# sticky toffee muffins

The addition of *dulce de leche*, which is rather like instant banoffee sauce, is a simple idea but makes these muffins deliciously indulgent. The overall effect is impressive, and irresistible to the taste buds.

you will need

**300 g/10½ oz plain flour**

**100 g/3½ oz golden granulated sugar**

**2 tsp baking powder**

**pinch of salt**

**2 heaped tsp instant coffee**

**75 g/2¾ oz butter, melted**

**2 eggs**

**½ tsp vanilla extract**

**1 carton (284 ml/10 fl oz) buttermilk**

**4 tsp *dulce de leche***

**12 chocolate-coated coffee beans, to decorate**

***dulce de leche*, to serve**

1 Preheat the oven to 190°/375°F/Gas Mark 5. Line a 10- or 12-hole non-stick muffin tray with paper cases.

2 Sift together the dry ingredients. Stir the coffee into the warm melted butter to blend. Whisk together the eggs, vanilla extract, buttermilk, *dulce de leche* and cooled butter mixture in a large mixing bowl. Quickly stir the dry ingredients into the whisked mixture, but don't try to blend smoothly; the batter should be a little lumpy.

3 Spoon the batter into the prepared cases almost to the top. Transfer to the oven and bake for about 20 minutes, or until the muffin tops are well risen and springy to the touch. Remove the muffins from the oven and allow to cool in the tray for 5 minutes, then transfer to a wire rack. Top each muffin with a chocolate-coated coffee bean and serve with *dulce de leche*.

# chocolate swirl muffins

These delicious muffins, made with dark and white chocolate and a hint of vanilla, are deeply decadent and yet surprisingly quick to make. They are the ideal choice for chocolate lovers.

## makes 10–12

**you will need**

oil, for greasing

300 g/10½ oz plain flour

150 g/5½ oz granulated sugar

2 tsp baking powder

pinch of salt

75 g/2¾ oz butter

75 g/2¾ oz dark chocolate, broken into pieces

75 g/2¾ oz white chocolate, broken into pieces

2 eggs, lightly beaten

1 tsp vanilla extract

sifted icing sugar and cocoa powder, to decorate

1   Preheat the oven to 190°C/375°F/Gas Mark 5. Lightly grease a 10- or 12-hole non-stick muffin tray (or 2 mini-muffin trays) or line with paper cases.

2   Sift together the dry ingredients and set aside. Put half the butter and the dark chocolate in a small heatproof bowl over a pan of gently simmering water to melt on a low heat. Put the rest of the butter and the white chocolate in a second small heatproof bowl and melt in the same way (you can do one after the other). Set aside both bowls when melted.

3   Meanwhile, beat together the eggs and vanilla. Stir in the melted white chocolate and butter. Add the dry mixture and lightly stir until just incorporated. Put one dessertspoonful of the mixture into each muffin case. Stir the cooled dark chocolate into the remaining batter and lightly swirl to give a marble effect, then spoon into the cases. You can give an extra swirl to the two coloured batters if you wish. Bake for 20 minutes, or until a skewer inserted in the centre comes out clean.

4   Remove the muffins from the oven and cool in the tray for 5 minutes, then transfer to a wire rack. Once cooled, decorate with sifted icing sugar and cocoa powder.

# marzipan muffins

There's not much added sugar in these muffins, but don't forget that the marzipan is very sweet, and so are the dried figs. The almond extract complements the marzipan flavour beautifully.

## makes 10–12

### you will need

oil, for greasing

200 g/7 oz plain flour

100 g/3½ oz granulated sugar

2 tsp baking powder

pinch of salt

2 small eggs

½ tsp almond extract

1 carton (284 ml/10 fl oz) buttermilk

125 ml/4 fl oz semi-skimmed milk

75 g/2¾ oz butter, melted

75 g/2¾ oz dried figs (ready to eat), chopped small

75 g/2¾ oz marzipan, coarsely grated

1   Preheat the oven to 200°C/400°F/Gas Mark 6. Lightly grease a 10- or 12-hole non-stick muffin tray or line with paper cases.

2   Sift together the dry ingredients. Whisk the eggs, almond extract, buttermilk, milk and butter together in a large mixing bowl. Add the chopped figs and marzipan and lightly mix through with your fingers, as if rubbing in pastry. Quickly stir the whisked mixture into the dry ingredients, but don't try to blend smoothly; the batter should be lumpy.

3   Spoon the batter into the prepared tray or cases almost to the top. Transfer to the oven and bake for about 20 minutes, or until the muffins tops are well risen and springy to the touch. Test one by inserting a skewer into the centre to check it comes out clean.

4   Remove the muffins from the oven and allow to cool in the tray for 5 minutes, then transfer to a wire rack.

# spiced orange muffins

These muffins use Christmas spices for people who find the traditional pudding too heavy. Topped with icing, they are sweet enough to appeal to children; adults will equally find room for one, or maybe two.

**makes 12**

**you will need**

4 tbsp vegetable oil, plus extra for greasing

300 g/10½ oz plain flour

150 g/5½ oz soft brown sugar

2 tsp baking powder

½ tsp bicarbonate of soda

¼ tsp salt

6 green cardamon pods, husks removed, seeds powdered

½ tsp ground cinnamon or cloves

zest and juice of 1 orange

125 ml/4 fl oz semi-skimmed milk

1 large egg

1 heaped tbsp orange marmalade, medium cut

**to decorate**

115 g/4 oz icing sugar

2–3 tsp water or lemon juice

silver dragées

1 Preheat the oven to 200°C/400°F/Gas Mark 6. Lightly grease two non-stick muffin trays or line with paper cases.

2 Sift the dry ingredients and spices together twice into a large bowl. In a second bowl, beat together the orange zest and juice, oil, milk, egg and marmalade, stirring well. Add to the dry mixture, stirring just to incorporate.

3 Spoon the batter into the prepared tray or cases almost to the top. Transfer to the oven and bake for about 15 minutes, or until the muffin tops are well risen and springy to the touch. Test one by inserting a skewer into the centre to check it comes out clean.

4 Remove the muffins from the oven and allow to cool in the tray for 5 minutes, then transfer to a wire rack.

5 Meanwhile, make the icing. Sift the icing sugar into a bowl. Add the water and stir until smooth and thick enough to coat the back of a wooden spoon. Spoon the icing on top of each muffin and decorate with silver dragées.

# decorating ideas

Few of us would go as far as to decorate freshly baked muffins – after all, they don't stay around for long out of the oven – but if you are making them ahead it can be charming to extend the homemade touch.

Muffins don't need dressing up but sometimes it's fun to add a finishing touch for a special event. You can personalise them with coloured-icing writing, adding names or numbers for young children (involve the kids in the process) or drizzle chocolate, zig-zag fashion, for a jazzy effect. I've cooked heart-shaped muffins for the family and sprinkled tiny ones with sugar crystals that sparkle – irresistible to little girls!

Chopped nuts or toasted desiccated coconut give a stylish presentation. You can make a quick glacé icing by sifting 115 g/4 oz icing sugar and blending in 2–3 teaspoons of water or lemon juice. No need to worry about it remaining on top; in fact, if it runs down the muffin sides it looks very effective. Press in your decorations before the icing sets. Sweets, such as chocolate buttons or jellied fruit diamonds, meet the party requirement. Alternatively, you can make a butter icing by blending icing sugar with butter instead of liquid or, for a less-sweet version, with cream cheese, carrot-cake fashion. I've made a similar version for savoury muffins, combining creamed horseradish with cream cheese and herbs.

 A slightly more sophisticated decoration is to top your muffins with chocolate ganache, which is foolproof: simply melt together

equal amounts of double cream and chocolate in a heatproof bowl over simmering water. It gives a lovely glossy topping that doesn't set as hard as chocolate alone.

Finally, you can have fun making muffins in different sizes: chunky ones that are almost a meal in themselves for lunch or a picnic, medium or mini ones for breakfast, coffee break or teatime. You can make a couple of batches in three different sizes and stack them for an impressive display. Or try giving a single muffin, presented beautifully in a box tied with ribbon or raffia, for a personal and very thoughtful gift.

# index

acknowledgements

Bright Ideas,
38 High Street,
Lewes,
East Sussex BN7 2LU

Monsieur Canelle et
Compagnon,
The Old Needlemakers,
West Street,
Lewes,
East Sussex BN7 2NZ

Revive-all,
The Old Needlemakers,
West Street,
Lewes,
East Sussex BN7 2NZ

Steamer Trading,
20/21 High Street,
Lewes,
East Sussex BN7 2BY